THE LITTLE BOOK OF
DOG
PHRENOLOGY

RP Minis™
Hachette Book Group
1290 Avenue of the Americas, New York, NY 10104
www.runningpress.com
@Running_Press

First Edition: May 2021

Published by RP Minis, an imprint of Perseus Books, LLC, a subsidiary of Hachette Book Group, Inc. The RP Minis name and logo is a trademark of the Hachette Book Group.

The Hachette Speakers Bureau provides a wide range of authors for speaking events. To find out more, go to www. hachettespeakersbureau.com or call (866) 376-6591.

The publisher is not responsible for websites (or their content) that are not owned by the publisher.

ISBN: 978-0-7624-7266-6

≡ CONTENTS ≡

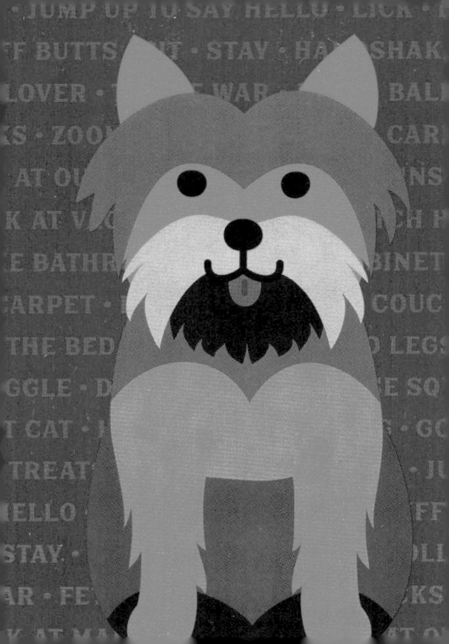

UNDERSTANDING
YOUR DOG

Have you ever wondered what goes
on inside your dog's head? Like why
she has to greet you with a toy every
time you walk in the door? Or why
he gives you sad eyes as soon as
you pack a travel bag? What exactly
is going through her mind as she
follows you from room to room while
you clean the house?

We're well aware of the things that all dogs seem to do like begging for food, barking at mail carriers, and requesting pats. And it goes without question that dogs are one of the sillier, floppier, yet more emotionally intelligent pets a person can have. So, what motivations exist behind their benevolent behavior? How do they know it's secretly okay to forego the rules of jumping onto the couch to sit with you after a bad day? And, most importantly, why are they so darn innocent? Some cat owners

may disagree, but dogs might have
more intricacies to them and
their behavior than what
meets the eye.

PHRENOLOGY:
A MINI HISTORY

•••• ▬ ••••

To figure out just how your pup ticks, it may be beneficial to take a look at the popular 19th and 20th centuries pseudoscience known as Phrenology.

Viennese doctor, Franz-Joseph Gall (1758-1828), developed Phrenology by studying the different shapes of human skulls in order to determine behavior. He and other doctors like Johann Spurzheim (1776-1832) believed that such study would provide insight to a person's behavior, and would help not only scientists, but average people to better understand each other.

Doctors who studied Phrenology would take what they learned from a human skull and map out specific regions on a model where certain "faculties" or behaviors existed in the brain. Gall and his contemporaries achieved this by documenting traits like: "adhesiveness" (friendship), "cautiousness," "combativeness," "ideality" (or love of excess), and "love of life."

DOG
PHRENOLOGY

..... 🦴 .....

What if we were able to apply the Phrenology basics to our most faithful and floofy friends? In doing so, we just may be able to uncover some hidden truths and allow owners to form an even deeper bond with their best friend.

The porcelain phrenology bust included with this guide will serve as a visual aid to help you better understand your dog's brain from the slobbery kisses, requests for belly rubs, and, of course, all the borks, yips, and awoos.

Our study has broken down a basic structure applicable to most dogs which include: Food, Friendliness, Obedience, Playfulness, Vigilance, Retaliation, Spatial Awareness, and Quirkiness.

Before we dive in, please keep in mind, none of this has been scientifically proven.

FOOD

·····◆·····

Food is a top, if not *the* top, priority for dogs. You've probably noticed how he tends to poke his head lovingly between your arms at the dinner table in order to snag a quick taste of your plate. Or that incredibly sad look she gives you as if she hadn't just been fed moments before you sat down. And don't even get us started on treats. Here are a few sections of the dog's brain as it relates to food:

BEG

GOBBLE FOOD

GET TREATS

BEG FOR
MORE FOOD

FRIENDLINESS

•••••◇•••••

As a dog parent, you've probably noticed that most dogs come in two varieties: pretty friendly and extra friendly. Due to their pack mentality, most dogs enjoy being around people and will be a friend to all, especially if it means getting extra pats and treats. Key sections of friendliness include:

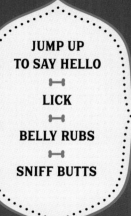

JUMP UP
TO SAY HELLO

LICK

BELLY RUBS

SNIFF BUTTS

OBEDIENCE

•••••◇•••••

There is no doubt that dogs are smart. When trained from an early age, dogs have the ability to learn a wide variety of things. Often swayed by treats and repetition, dogs can learn tricks and even assist those in need as service animals. Some sections deep within a dog's brain associated with obedience are:

SIT

STAY

HANDSHAKE OR PAW

ROLLOVER

PLAYFULNESS

•••••◆•••••

When you return home from work, does your dog run around the house barking in excitement, signaling that it's time to play? Or does she jump on top of you while you're practicing yoga? You've probably noticed your dog is ready to play at almost any moment if you're willing to. Parts of your dog's brain that guide this behavior are:

TUG OF WAR

FETCH BALLS

FETCH STICKS

ZOOMIES

VIGILANCE

······◆······

Of course, dogs are not always just fun and games. They hold a deep desire to protect their humans from harm or intruders, and it often feels like they are always ready to protect you from any sort of impending doom. These traits include:

BARK AT MAIL CARRIERS

BARK AT OUTSIDE NOISE

BARK AT INSIDE NOISE

BARK AT VACUUM CLEANER

RETALIATION

•••••◆••••••

As you probably know, your dog will always let you know when they have beef with you—well, maybe not actual beef. They like to take deliberate action when communicating their desire for more walks and food or their displeasure at being left home alone for hours. Sometimes, they pout around you, and other times, they destroy your slippers. Dogs express when they're displeased through behaviors like:

CHEW ON CABINETS

⊢•⊣

PEE ON THE CARPET

⊢•⊣

DIG A HOLE IN THE COUCH

SPATIAL
AWARENESS

····◇·····

If your dog has tried to "curl up" into
your lap or squeeze into a space that
they don't belong, then you probably
already know that dogs are not
the best with spatial awareness.
Their overwhelming need to be on or
near you at all times overwhelms the
part of their brain that tells them,
"hey, you aren't going to fit there."
Behaviors like this are:

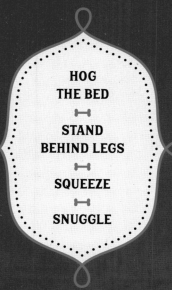

HOG
THE BED

STAND
BEHIND LEGS

SQUEEZE

SNUGGLE

QUIRKINESS

····◇·····

There's no denying that your dog has some quirks. What you might not know is that most stem from his or her wolf-like ancestry. Many of these traits are buried deep in instinct, but that doesn't mean that sometimes they don't come off as incredibly silly or questionable. Some quirky behaviors include:

DESTROY TOYS

CHASE SQUIRRELS

TAUNT THE CAT

HOWL AT SIRENS

FOR THE LOVE OF
DOGS

••••• 🦴 •••••

It is hard to ignore the unbreakable bond between humans and dogs. They snuggle us when we're sick, goof off when we're sad, and make the best companions around. Even when they're getting under foot or barking too loud, they always have us in mind. They are utterly devoted to being our best friends and the feeling is always mutual. While we may not entirely know what's going on in their brains or why specific quirks exist, we hope that *Phrenology Dog* has given you a baseline to help

you better understand your best girl or boy. And if one day you find your dog howling along to sounds from the great outdoors, remember to check the dog brain!

This book has been bound
using handcraft methods
and Smyth-sewn to
ensure durability.

•••••◆•••••

The box and interior were
designed by Susan Van Horn.

•••••◆•••••

Illustrations created from
artwork by ayutaka from the
Getty Images Plus collection.

•••••◆•••••

The text was written
by Brenna Dinon.